STATUTORY INSTRUMENTS

1992 No. 3147

SOCIAL SECURITY
HOUSING, ENGLAND AND WALES
HOUSING, SCOTLAND

The Social Security Benefits (Amendments Consequential Upon the Introduction of Community Care) Regulations 1992

Made	10th December 1992
Laid before Parliament	15th December 1992
Coming into force	1st April 1993

The Secretary of State for Social Security, in exercise of the powers conferred by sections 67(2), 72(8), 123(1), 130(2) and (4), 135(1), 137(1) and (2)(h) and (i) and 175(1) to (5) of the Social Security Contributions and Benefits Act 1992(a), and sections 5(1)(q), 73(1)(b) and 189(1) to (6) of the Social Security Administration Act 1992(b), and of all other powers enabling him in that behalf, so far as these Regulations relate to housing benefit, after consultation with organisations appearing to him to be representative of the authorities concerned(c), and after reference to the Social Security Advisory Committee(d), hereby makes the following Regulations:

PART I

GENERAL

Citation, commencement and interpretation

1.—(1) These Regulations may be cited as the Social Security Benefits (Amendments Consequential Upon the Introduction of Community Care) Regulations 1992 and shall come into force on 1st April 1993.

(2) In these Regulations–
"the Income Support Regulations" means the Income Support (General) Regulations 1987(e);

(a) 1992 c.4; section 137(1) is an interpretation provision and is cited because of the meaning ascribed to the word "prescribed".
(b) 1992 c.5.
(c) *See* section 176(1) of the Social Security Administration Act 1992.
(d) *See* section 172(1) of the Social Security Administration Act 1992.
(e) S.I. 1987/1967.

"the Housing Benefit Regulations" means the Housing Benefit (General) Regulations 1987(a).

(3) In these Regulations, unless the context otherwise requires, a reference–
  (a) to a numbered Part is to the Part of these Regulations bearing that number;
  (b) to a numbered regulation or Schedule is to the regulation or Schedule to these Regulations bearing that number; and
  (c) in a regulation or Schedule to a numbered paragraph is to the paragraph in that regulation or Schedule bearing that number.

PART II

INCOME SUPPORT

Introduction of Residential Allowance

2.—(1) In the Income Support Regulations–
  (a) in paragraph (1) of regulation 2 (interpretation), there shall be inserted at the appropriate places–
    ""preserved right" means a preserved right for the purpose of regulation 19;
    "residential allowance" means the weekly amount determined in accordance with paragraph 2A of Schedule 2;";
  (b) in paragraph (1) of regulation 17 (applicable amounts), after sub-paragraph (b), there shall be inserted the following sub-paragraph–
    "(bb) an amount in respect of himself, or where the claimant is a member of a family, an amount in respect of any member of the family aged 16 or over, determined in accordance with paragraph 2A of Schedule 2 (residential allowance);";
  (c) in paragraph (1) of regulation 18(b) (polygamous marriages), after sub-paragraph (c), there shall be inserted the following sub-paragraph–
    "(cc) an amount, whether in respect of the claimant or any member of his household aged 16 or over, determined in accordance with paragraph 2A of Schedule 2 (residential allowance);"; and
  (d) in Part I of Schedule 2, after paragraph 2, there shall be inserted the following paragraph–
    " 2A.—(1) The weekly amount for the purposes of regulation 17(1)(bb) and 18(1)(cc) (residential allowance) in respect of a person who satisfies the conditions specified in sub-paragraph (2) shall be–
      (a) except in a case to which head (b) applies, £45.00; and
      (b) where the home in which the person resides is situated within the area described in Schedule 3C (the Greater London area), £50.00.
    (2) Subject to sub-paragraphs (3) and (4), the conditions are–
      (a) the person resides in a residential care home or a nursing home and for this purpose a person shall be regarded as residing in such a home during any period of absence from the home which does not exceed 6 days;
      (b) he does not have a preserved right;
      (c) he is aged 16 or over;
      (d) both the person's accommodation and such meals (if any) as are provided for him are provided on a commercial basis; and
      (e) no part of the weekly charge for accommodation is met by housing benefit.

(a) S.I. 1987/1971.
(b) The relevant amending instrument is S.I. 1988/1228.

(3) For the purposes of sub-paragraph (2), but subject to sub-paragraph (4), a person resides in a residential care home where the home in which he resides–
  (a) is registered under Part I of the Registered Homes Act 1984(a) or is deemed to be so registered by virtue of section 2(3) of the Registered Homes (Amendment) Act 1991(b) (registration of small homes where application for registration not determined);
  (b) is managed or provided by a body incorporated by Royal Charter or constituted by Act of Parliament (other than a social services authority) and provides both board and personal care for the claimant; or
  (c) is in Scotland and is registered under section 61 of the Social Work (Scotland) Act 1968(c) or is an establishment provided by a housing association registered with Scottish Homes established by the Housing (Scotland) Act 1988(d) which provides care equivalent to that given in residential accommodation provided under Part IV of the Social Work (Scotland) Act 1968;

and a person resides in a nursing home where the home in which he resides is such a home for the purposes of regulation 19.

(4) A person shall not be regarded as residing in a nursing home for the purposes of sub-paragraph (2) where the home in which he resides is a hospice, and for this purpose "hospice" means a nursing home which–
  (a) if situate in England or Wales, is registered under Part II of the Registered Homes Act 1984, or
  (b) if situate in Scotland, is exempted from the operation of the Nursing Homes Registration (Scotland) Act 1938 by virtue of section 6 of that Act (e),

and which provides nursing for persons resident therein who suffer from a progressive disease and for whom the purpose of treatment is palliative.

(5) Where–
  (a) a person has been registered under the Registered Homes Act 1984 in respect of premises which have been carried on as a residential care home or, as the case may be, a nursing home, and that person has ceased to carry on such a home; and
  (b) an application for registration under that Act has been made by another person and that application has not been determined or abandoned,

then any question arising for determination under this paragraph shall be determined as if the most recent registration under that Act in respect of those premises continued until the day on which the application is determined or abandoned.".

(2) Schedule 1, which contains amendments of the Income Support Regulations consequential upon the introduction of a residential allowance, shall have effect.

(3) Schedule 2, which inserts a new Schedule 3C into the Income Support Regulations, shall also have effect.

Preserved rights

3.—(1) In regulation 19 of the Income Support Regulations (applicable amounts for persons in residential care and nursing homes)–
  (a) in paragraph (1), for the words preceding the words "his weekly applicable amount", there shall be substituted the words–

(a) 1984 c.23.
(b) 1991 c.20.
(c) 1968 c.49; section 61 was amended by the Criminal Procedure (Scotland) Act 1975 (c.21) section 289c and g and Schedule 7c.
(d) 1988 c.43.
(e) 1938 c.73.

" (1) Subject to regulation 22 (reduction of applicable amounts) where a claimant has a preserved right and either–
- (a) lives in a residential care or nursing home; or
- (b) is a member of a family and he and the members of his family live in such a home,";

(b) after paragraph (1ZA)(a) there shall be inserted the following paragraphs–

" (1ZB) In this regulation a person has a preserved right, subject to paragraphs (1ZE) and (1ZF), where–
- (a) on 31st March 1993, he was living in a residential care home or a nursing home, and–
  - (i) was entitled to income support for the benefit week in which that day fell and his applicable amount was calculated in accordance with Part I of Schedule 4; or
  - (ii) was not in that week entitled to income support because he was able to meet the cost of the accommodation from other sources available to him, but subsequently becomes entitled to income support; or
- (b) he would have been living in a residential care home or nursing home on 31st March 1993 but for an absence which, including that day, does not exceed–
  - (i) except in a case to which head (ii) applies–
    - (aa) where the person was before his absence a temporary resident in the home, 4 weeks, or
    - (bb) where the person was before his absence a permanent resident in the home, 13 weeks; or
  - (ii) where throughout the period of absence the person was a patient, 52 weeks,

and the provisions of sub-paragraph (a) would have applied to him but for that absence.

(1ZC) Subject to paragraphs (1ZD), (1ZE) and (1ZF), a person also has a preserved right where–
- (a) on 31st March 1993 he was living in a residential care home or nursing home within the meaning of paragraph (3) as then in force, and was entitled to income support but his applicable amount was not calculated in accordance with Part I of Schedule 4 because he was a person to whom paragraph 14 of Schedule 4 applied(b) (accommodation provided by a close relative); and
- (b) after 31st March 1993, either–
  - (i) he moved from the home in which he was residing on that date to another residential care home or nursing home, or
  - (ii) the ownership of the home changed,

and in the home to which he moved, or as the case may be, following the change of ownership, the accommodation and meals (if any) are provided for him by a person other than a close relative of his or by any member of his family, and are provided on a commercial basis.

(1ZD) Where a person has a preserved right under paragraph (1ZC), that right shall commence on the first full day of residence in the residential care home or nursing home to which he moved, or as the case may be, the day after the ownership of the property changed.

(1ZE) A person does not have a preserved right by virtue of paragraph (1ZB)(a)(ii) or (1ZC) where the residential care home in which he was living provided both board and personal care for less than 4 persons.

(a) Paragraph (1ZA) was inserted by S.I. 1991/1033.
(b) Paragraph 14 was substituted by regulation 31(b) of S.I. 1988/663.

(1ZF) Paragraphs (1ZB) and (1ZC) shall cease to apply to a person who has a preserved right where he is absent from a residential care home or nursing home and that absence exceeds a period of–
- (a) except in a case to which sub-paragraph (b) applies–
  - (i) 4 weeks, where the person was before his absence a temporary resident in the home, or,
  - (ii) 13 weeks, where the person was before his absence a permanent resident in the home; or
- (b) 52 weeks where throughout the period of absence the person was a patient.

(1ZG) (a) A person who acquired a preserved right under paragraph (1ZB) or (1ZC) shall cease to have that right where either–
  - (i) he moves from the home he resided in, or would but for an absence specified in paragraph (1ZB)(b) have resided in, on 31st March 1993 to another residential care home or nursing home, or
  - (ii) the ownership of that home changes;

and in the home to which he moves or, as the case may be, following the change of ownership, the accommodation and meals (if any) are provided for him by a close relative of his, or by a member of his family, and are provided otherwise than on a commercial basis;

(b) a preserved right acquired under paragraph (1ZB) or (1ZC) which ceased to apply to a person in accordance with sub-paragraph (a) shall, notwithstanding that paragraph, revive and again apply in his case where–
  - (i) he moves from the home mentioned in sub-paragraph (a)(i) to another residential care home or nursing home, or
  - (ii) the ownership of that home changes, or in the case of a home mentioned in sub-paragraph (a)(ii), changes again,

and in the home to which he moves or, as the case may be, following the change or further change of ownership, the accommodation and meals (if any) are provided for him otherwise than by a close relative of his, or by a member of his family, and are provided on a commercial basis.

(1ZH) For the purposes of paragraphs (1ZB) and (1ZF) a person is a permanent resident in a residential care home or nursing home where the home is his principal place of abode, and a temporary resident where it is not.

(1ZJ) For the avoidance of doubt, the expression "residential care home" in paragraphs (1ZB) and (1ZE) has the meaning it bore on 31st March 1993.".

PART III

HOUSING BENEFIT

Amendment of regulation 5 of the Housing Benefit Regulations

4. In regulation 5 of the Housing Benefit Regulations (circumstances in which a person is or is not to be treated as occupying a dwelling as his home)**(a)**, in paragraph (9), in the definition of "residential accommodation"–

(a) Relevant amending instrument is S.I. 1988/1971.

(a) for sub-paragraph (a) there shall be substitued the following sub-paragraph–

"(a) under sections 21 to 24 and 26 of the National Assistance Act 1948**(a)** (provision of accommodation) where–

(i) board is available to the claimant, and

(ii) the home in which the accommodation is provided is either owned or managed or owned and managed by a local authority, and;";

(b) sub-paragraph (b) shall be omitted;

(c) for sub-paragraph (c) there shall be substituted the following sub-paragraph–

"(c) under section 59 of the Social Work (Scotland) Act 1968**(b)** (provision of residential and other establishments) where–

(i) board is available to the claimant, and

(ii) the home in which the accommodation is provided is either owned or managed or owned and managed by a local authority, and;";

(d) after sub-paragraph (j), there shall be added the following sub-paragraph–

"(k) in sub-paragraphs (a) and (c), "board" refers to the availability to the claimant in the home in which his accommodation is provided of cooked or prepared food, where the food is made available to him in consequence solely of his paying the charge for the accommodation or any charge which he is required to pay as a result of occupying the accommodation, or both of those charges, and is made available for his consumption without any further charge to him;".

Amendment of regulation 7 of the Housing Benefit Regulations

5.—(1) Regulation 7 of the Housing Benefit Regulations (circumstances in which a person is to be treated as not liable to make payments in respect of a dwelling)**(c)** shall be amended in accordance with the following provisions of this regulation.

(2) In paragraph (2), sub-paragraphs (a) and (b) shall be omitted.

(3) After paragraph (3) there shall be added the following paragraphs–

"(4) Subject to the following provisions of this regulation, paragraph (5) applies to a person who–

(a) occupies or is treated by regulation 5(8) as occupying residential accommodation on 31st March 1993,

(b) is or was liable to pay rent in respect of that accommodation for that day,

(c) is a person to whom sub-paragraph (a) or (b) of paragraph (2) applies immediately before 1st April 1993; and

(d) is or was entitled to housing benefit in respect of the liability mentioned in sub-paragraph (b).

(5) In the case of a person to whom this paragraph applies, regulation 7 shall continue to apply to him as if the amendments specified in regulation 5(2) of the Social Security Benefits (Amendments Consequential Upon the Introduction of Community Care) Regulations 1992**(d)** had not been made.

(6) Subject to the following provisions of this regulation, paragraph (7) applies to a person who–

(a) occupies or is treated under regulation 5(8) as occupying accommodation in an establishment which on 1st April 1993 is registered as a small home under Part I of the Registered Homes Act 1984**(e)** or is deemed to be so registered under section 2(3) of the Registered Homes (Amendment) Act 1991**(f)** (registration of small homes where application for registration not determined);

(a) 1948 c.29; section 21 is amended by the National Health Service and Community Care Act 1990 (c.19) section 42(1); section 26 is amended by section 42(2) to (6) of the same Act.
(b) 1968 c.49.
(c) Regulation 7 was amended by S.I. 1990/2564.
(d) S.I. 1992/3147.
(e) 1984 c.23.
(f) 1991 c.20.

(b) was occupying, or was treated under regulation 5(8) as occupying, that accommodation on 31st March 1993;

(c) is or was liable to pay rent in respect of that accommodation for 31st March 1993; and

(d) is or was entitled to housing benefit in respect of that liability.

(7) In the case of a person to whom this paragraph applies, paragraph (3) shall apply as if sub-paragraph (a) was omitted.

(8) Subject to paragraph (9), where on 1st April 1993 paragraph (5) or paragraph (7) applies to a person that paragraph shall cease to apply to him–

(a) on the day on which he is first absent from the accommodation which he occupied or was treated under regulation 5(8) as occupying on 31st March 1993; and

(b) on any day which falls after that day.

(9) For the purposes of paragraph (8) any absence which is temporary shall be disregarded and for those purposes an absence is temporary where during the absence the person is treated by regulation 5(8) as occupying the accommodation as his home.

(10) Where a person–

(a) ceases to be entitled to housing benefit; and

(b) was before he ceased to be entitled a person to whom either paragraph (5) or paragraph (7) applied,

that paragraph or those paragraphs shall not apply to him in the case of any subsequent claim for housing benefit except where the claim takes effect in accordance with regulation 72(12) or (13) (repeat claims) immediately after the end of the benefit period.

(11) Where on 31st March 1993 a person occupies or is treated as occupying an establishment mentioned in paragraph (6)(a) and on a day subsequent to that date the establishment–

(a) if it was registered under Part I of the Registered Homes Act 1984, ceases to be so registered; or

(b) if it was deemed to be so registered is neither registered nor deemed to be registered,

then on that day and on any day thereafter paragraph (7) shall not apply to that person.

(12) In this regulation, "small home" has the same meaning as in Part I of the Registered Homes Act 1984(a) by virtue of section 1(4A) of that Act(b).".

Amendment of regulation 8 of the Housing Benefit Regulations

6.—(1) In regulation 8 of the Housing Benefit Regulations (eligible housing costs)(c) in paragraph (2)–

(a) in sub-paragraph (a) after the words "for that benefit includes" there shall be inserted the words "a residential allowance or"; and

(b) for sub-paragraph (b), there shall be substituted the following sub-paragraph–

"(b) payments in respect of accommodation provided under–

(i) sections 21 to 24 and 26 of the National Assistance Act 1948(d) where–

(aa) board is available to the claimant, and

(bb) the home in which the accommodation is provided is either owned or managed or owned and managed by a local authority; or

---

(a) 1984 c.23.
(b) Inserted by section 1(2) of the Registered Homes (Amendment) Act 1991 (c.20).
(c) The relevant amending instruments are S.I. 1988/1444, 1971 and 1992/201.
(d) 1948 c.29; section 21 is amended by the National Health Service and Community Care Act 1990 (c.19) section 42(1); section 26 is amended by section 42(2) to (6) of the same Act.

>   (ii) in Scotland, section 59 of the Social Work (Scotland) Act 1968**(a)** where–
>   - (aa) board is available to the claimant, and
>   - (bb) the home in which the accommodation is provided is either owned or managed or owned and managed by a local authority;
>
> and for these purposes "board" refers to the availability to the claimant in the home in which his accommodation is provided of cooked or prepared food, where the food is made available to him in consequence solely of his paying the charge for the accommodation or any other charge which he is required to pay as a condition of occupying the accommodation, or both of those charges, and is made available for his consumption without any further charge to him;".

PART IV

DISABILITY BENEFITS

7.—(1) In regulation 9 of the Social Security (Disability Living Allowance) Regulations 1991**(b)** ("the Disability Living Allowance Regulations") (persons in certain accommodation other than hospitals), paragraph (3) shall be omitted.

(2) In regulation 10 of those Regulations (which relates to persons in hospital and certain other accommodation)–

- (a) in paragraph (1), for the words "subject to paragraphs (2) and (3)" there shall be substituted the words "subject to the following provisions of this regulation";
- (b) after paragraph (5), there shall be inserted the following paragraphs–

    > "(6) Regulation 8 or as the case may be regulation 9 shall not apply in the case of a person who is residing in a hospice and is terminally ill where the Secretary of State has been informed that he is terminally ill–
    >   - (a) on a claim for the care component,
    >   - (b) on an application for a review of an award of disability living allowance, or
    >   - (c) in writing in connection with an award of, or a claim for, or an application for a review of an award of, disability living allowance.
    >
    > (7) In paragraph (6) "hospice" means a hospital or other institution other than–
    >   - (a) a health service hospital (within the meaning of section 128 of the NHS Act of 1977**(c)**) in England or Wales;
    >   - (b) a health service hospital (within the meaning of section 108(1) of the NHS Act of 1978**(d)**) in Scotland;
    >   - (c) a hospital maintained or administered by the Defence Council; or
    >   - (d) an institution similar to a hospital mentioned in any of the preceding sub-paragraphs of this paragraph.
    >
    > (8) Regulation 9 shall not apply in any particular case for any period during which–
    >   - (a) the person for whom the accommodation is provided–
    >   - (i) is not entitled to income support,
    >   - (ii) is not entitled to housing benefit, or

(a) 1968 c.49.
(b) S.I. 1992/2890; regulation 9 is amended by S.I. 1992/2869.
(c) 1977 c.49; section 128 was amended by paragraph 77(d) of Schedule 1 to the Health Services Act 1980 (c.53) and section 26(2)(c) of the National Health Service and Community Care Act 1990 (c.19).
(d) 1978 c.29; section 108(1) was amended by paragraph 19(22)(b) of Schedule 9 to the National Health Service and Community Care Act 1990.

(iii) is not a member of a married or unmarried couple for whom an amount is included for income support purposes in the weekly applicable amount of the other member, and
(b) the whole of the cost of that accommodation is met–
(i) out of the person's own resources, or partly out of his own resources and partly with assistance from another person or a charity; or
(ii) on his behalf by another person or a charity.".

(3) Where a person has a preserved right, regulations 9 and 10 of the Disability Living Allowance Regulations shall apply in his case as if the amendments set out in paragraphs (1) and (2) of this regulation had not been made.

(4) For the purposes of paragraph (3) but subject to paragraph (5) a person has a preserved right where–
(a) on 31st March 1993, he was living in a home registered under the Registered Homes Act 1984(a) as a residential care home or a nursing home; or
(b) he would have been living in such a home on that date but for an absence which, including that day, does not exceed–
(i) except in a case to which head (ii) applies–
(aa) where the person was before his absence a temporary resident in the home, 4 weeks, or
(bb) where the person was before his absence a permanent resident in the home, 13 weeks, or
(ii) where throughout the period of his absence he was receiving free hospital treatment within the meaning of the Social Security (Hospital In-Patients) Regulations 1975(b), 52 weeks.

(5) Paragraphs (3) and (4) shall cease to apply to a person who has a preserved right where he is absent from a home such as is mentioned in paragraph (3)(a) and that absence exceeds a period of–
(a) except in a case to which sub-paragraph (b) applies–
(i) 4 weeks, where the person was before his absence a temporary resident in the home, or
(ii) 13 weeks, where the person was before his absence a permanent resident in the home; or
(b) 52 weeks where throughout the period of absence the person was receiving free in-patient treatment within the meaning of the Social Security (Hospital In-Patients) Regulations 1975.

(6) For the purposes of this regulation, a person is a permanent resident where the home in which he resides is his principal place of abode, and a temporary resident where it is not.

Amendments relating to attendance allowance

8.—(1) In regulation 7 of the Social Security (Attendance Allowance) Regulations 1991(c) ("the Attendance Allowance Regulations") (persons in certain accommodation other than hospitals), paragraph (2)(d) shall be omitted.

(2) In regulation 8 of those Regulations(e) (which relates to persons in hospitals and in certain other accommodation)–
(a) in paragraph (1), for the words "subject to paragraph (3)" there shall be substituted the words "subject to the following provisions of this regulation"; and

---

(a) 1984 c.23.
(b) *See* regulation 2(2) of S.I. 1975/555, as amended by S.I. 1987/1683.
(c) S.I. 1991/2740; the relevant amending instrument is S.I. 1992/703.
(d) Paragraph (2) was amended by S.I. 1992/703 and 2869.
(e) Regulation 8 was amended by S.I. 1992/703 and 2869.

(b) after paragraph (3), there shall be added the following paragraphs–

"(4) Regulation 6 or, as the case may be, regulation 7 shall not apply in the case of a person who is residing in a hospice and is terminally ill where the Secretary of State has been informed that he is terminally ill–

(a) on a claim for attendance allowance,

(b) on an application for a review of an award of attendance allowance, or

(c) in writing in connection with an award of, or a claim for, or an application for a review of an award of, attendance allowance.

(5) In paragraph (4) "hospice" means a hospital or other institution other than–

(a) a health service hospital (within the meaning of section 128 of the NHS Act of 1977(**a**)) in England or Wales;

(b) a health service hospital (within the meaning of section 108(1) of the NHS Act of 1978(**b**)) in Scotland;

(c) a hospital maintained or administered by the Defence Council; or

(d) an institution similar to a hospital mentioned in any of the preceding sub-paragraphs of this paragraph.

(6) Regulation 7 shall not apply in any particular case for any period during which–

(a) the person for whom the accommodation is provided–

(i) is not entitled to income support;

(ii) is not entitled to housing benefit; or

(iii) is not a member of a married or unmarried couple for whom an amount is included for income support purposes in the weekly applicable amount of the other member; and

(b) the whole of the cost of the accommodation is met–

(i) out of his own resources, or partly out of his own resources and partly with assistance from another person or a charity;

(ii) on his behalf by another person or a charity.".

(3) Where a person has a preserved right, regulations 7 and 8 of the Attendance Allowance Regulations shall apply in his case as if the amendments set out in paragraphs (1) and (2) of this regulation had not been made.

(4) For the purposes of paragraph (3) but subject to paragraph (5) a person has a preserved right where–

(a) on 31st March 1993, he was living in a home registered under the Registered Homes Act 1984(**c**) as a residential care home or a nursing home; or

(b) he would have been living in such a home on that date but for an absence which, including that day, does not exceed–

(i) except in a case to which head (ii) applies–

(aa) where the person was before his absence a temporary resident in the home, 4 weeks, or

(bb) where the person was before his absence a permanent resident in the home, 13 weeks, or

(ii) where throughout the period of his absence he was receiving free hospital treatment within the meaning of the Social Security (Hospital In-Patients) Regulations 1975(**d**), 52 weeks.

(**a**) 1977 c.49; section 128 was amended by paragraph 77(d) of Schedule 1 to the Health Services Act 1980 (c.53) and section 26(2)(c) of the National Health Service and Community Care Act 1990 (c.19).

(**b**) 1978 c.29; section 108(1) was amended by paragraph 19(22)(b) of Schedule 9 to the National Health Service and Community Care Act 1990.

(**c**) 1984 c.23.

(**d**) *See* regulation 2(2) of S.I. 1975/555, as amended by S.I. 1987/1683.

(5) Paragraphs (3) and (4) shall cease to apply to a person who has a preserved right where he is absent from a home such as is mentioned in paragraph (3)(a) and that absence exceeds a period of–
- (a) except in a case to which sub-paragraph (b) applies–
  - (i) 4 weeks, where the person was before his absence a temporary resident in the home, or
  - (ii) 13 weeks, where the person was before his absence a permanent resident in the home; or
- (b) 52 weeks where throughout the period of absence the person was receiving free in-patient treatment within the meaning of the Social Security (Hospital In-Patients) Regulations 1975(a).

(6) For the purposes of this regulation, a person is a permanent resident where the home in which he resides is his principal place of abode, and a temporary resident where it is not.

Signed by authority of the Secretary of State for Social Security.

10th December 1992

Alistair Burt
Parliamentary Under-Secretary of State,
Department of Social Security

(a) *See* regulation 2(2) of S.I. 1975/555, as amended by S.I. 1987/1683.

SCHEDULE 1

Regulation 2(2)

AMENDMENTS CONSEQUENTIAL UPON THE INTRODUCTION OF COMMUNITY CARE

1. In regulation 16 of the Income Support Regulations (circumstances in which a person is to be treated as being or not being a member of the household), in paragraph (3), sub-paragraph (c) shall be omitted.

2. In regulation 19(3) of the Income Support Regulations (applicable amounts for persons in residential care and nursing homes), in the definition of "residential care home"–
- (a) in sub-paragraph (a) after the words "so registered" there shall be inserted the words ", or is deemed to be registered under section 2(3) of the Registered Homes (Amendment) Act 1991(a) (which refers to the registration of small homes where the application for registration has not been determined)";
- (b) sub-paragraph (b) shall be omitted; and
- (c) in sub-paragraph (e) for the words "a housing association registered with the Housing Corporation established by the Housing Act 1964", there shall be substituted the words "a housing association registered with Scottish Homes established by the Housing (Scotland) Act 1988(b)".

3. In regulation 21 of the Income Support Regulations (special cases)–
- (a) in paragraph (3), for the definition of "residential accommodation", there shall be substituted the following definition–

    ""residential accommodation" means, subject to the following provisions of this regulation, accommodation provided by a local authority in a home owned or managed by that or another local authority–
    - (a) under sections 21 to 24 and 26 of the National Assistance Act 1948(c) (provision of accommodation); or
    - (b) in Scotland, under section 13B or 59 of the Social Work (Scotland) Act 1968(d) (provision of residential and other establisments) other than in premises registered under section 61 of that Act (registration) and which are used for the rehabilitation of alcoholics or drug addicts; or
    - (c) under section 7 of the Mental Health (Scotland) Act 1984(e) (functions of local authorities),

    where the accommodation is provided for a person whose stay in that accommodation has become other than temporary.";
- (b) in paragraph (4), for the words "that person attained pensionable age", there shall be substituted the words–

    "that person attained pensionable age; or (c) for whom board is not provided."; and

---

(a) 1991 c.20.
(b) 1988 c.43.
(c) 1948 c.29; section 21 was amended by the Local Government Act 1972 (c.70), Schedule 23, paragraphs 1 and 2 and Schedule 30; the National Health Service Reorganisation Act 1973 (c.32), Schedule 4, paragraph 44 and Schedule 5; the Housing (Homeless Persons) Act 1977 (c.48), Schedule; the National Health Service Act 1977 (c.49), Schedule 15, paragraph 5; the Health Service Act 1980 (c.53), Schedule 1, Part I, paragraph 5; and the National Health Service and Community Care Act 1990 (c.19), section 42(1), Schedule 9, paragraph 5(1) and (2) and Schedule 10. Section 22 was amended by the Social Work (Scotland) Act 1968 (c.49), section 87(4) and Schedule 9, Part I; the Supplementary Benefits Act 1976 (c.71), Schedule 7, paragraph 3; the Housing (Homeless Persons) Act 1977 (c.48), Schedule; the Social Security Act 1980 (c.30), section 20, Schedule 4, paragraph 2(1) and Schedule 5, Part II; the Health and Social Services and Social Security Adjudication Act 1983 (c.41), section 20(1)(a), and the National Health Service and Community Care Act 1990, section 44, Schedule 10. Section 24 was amended by the National Assistance (Amendment) Act 1959 (c.30), section 1(1); the National Health Service (Scotland) Act 1972 (c.58), Schedule 6, paragraph 82; the Local Government Act 1972 (c.70), Schedule 23, paragraph 2; the National Health Service Reorganisation Act 1973 (c.32), Schedule 4, paragraph 45; the Housing (Homeless Persons) Act 1977 (c.48), Schedule, and the National Health Service and Community Care Act 1990, Schedule 9, paragraph 5(4). Section 26 was amended by the Health Services and Public Health Act 1968 (c.46), section 44 and Schedule 4 and the Social Work (Scotland) Act, 1968 (c.49) Schedule 9, Part I and applied by section 87(3); the Local Government Act 1972 (c.70), Schedule 23, paragraph 2; the Housing (Homeless Persons) Act 1977 (c.48), Schedule; the Health and Social Services and Social Security Adjudications Act 1983 (c.41), section 20(1)(b) and the National Health Service and Community Care Act 1990, section 42(2) to (5), Schedule 9, paragraph 5(5), and Schedule 10.
(d) 1968 c.49; section 13B is inserted by the National Health Service and Community Care Act 1990, section 56; section 59 is amended by the same Act of 1990, Schedule 9, paragraph 10(7).
(e) 1984 c.36.

(c) in paragraph (4A)**(a)** for the words "In paragraph (3), sub-paragraph (d)(i) in the definition of "residential accommodation", there shall be substituted the words "In paragraph (4), sub-paragraph (c)".

4. In regulation 71 of the Income Support Regulations (applicable amount in urgent cases), in sub-paragraph (c) of paragraph (1)–
  (a) in head (i) for the words "90 per cent" there shall be substituted the words "98 per cent"; and
  (b) head (iii) shall be omitted.

5. In Schedule 7 to the Income Support Regulations (applicable amounts in special cases) for the words "£54.15 of which £43.30 is in respect of accommodation and £10.85 for personal expenses", the words "£54.15 of which £10.85 is for personal expenses" shall be substituted in the second column of each of the following paragraphs–
  (a) 10A**(b)** (single claimants temporarily in local authority accommodation);
  (b) 10B(1), (2), (3) and (4)**(c)** (couples and members of polygamous marriages where one member is or all are temporarily in local authority accommodation);
  (c) 10C**(d)** (lone parents who are in residential accommodation temporarily); and
  (d) 13(1)(a) (persons in residential accommodation).

6. The following amendments shall also be made to Schedule 7 to the Income Support Regulations–
  (a) in paragraph 10A, the words "Except where paragraph 10B(4) applies" shall be omitted;
  (b) in paragraph 10B sub-paragraph (4) shall be omitted;
  (c) paragraph 10D**(e)** (lone parents who are in a residential care home or nursing home temporarily) shall be omitted; and
  (d) in column (1) of paragraph 16**(f)** for the words "any of sub-paragraphs (a) to (d) (excluding heads (i) and (ii) of sub-paragraph (d))", there shall be substituted the words "any of sub-paragraphs (a) to (c)".

7. In Schedule 9 to the Income Support Regulations (sums to be disregarded in the calculation of income other than earnings)–
  (a) in paragraph 15, in sub-paragraph (2), after the words "(persons in residential care or nursing homes)" there shall be inserted the words "or by a local authority under Part III of the National Assistance Act 1948**(g)**"; and
  (b) in paragraph 30, in sub-paragraph (d), after the words "(residential care and nursing homes)", there shall be inserted the words "or the amount payable by a local authority in accordance with Part III of the National Assistance Act 1948".

8.—(1) In paragraph 4(1) of Schedule 9 to the Social Security (Claims and Payments) Regulations 1987**(h)**, for the words preceding "the adjudicating authority may determine", there shall be substituted the words–

" **4.**—(1) Where an award of income support–
  (a) is made to a person in a residential care home or nursing home as defined in regulation 19(3) of the Income Support Regulations**(i)**, or
  (b) includes an amount under Schedule 4 (persons in residential care and nursing homes) or paragraph 13 (residential accommodation) or 13A (Polish resettlement) of Schedule 7 to the Income Support Regulations,
(hereafter in this paragraph referred to as "miscellaneous accommodation costs")".

(a) Paragraph (4A) was inserted by S.I. 1992/2158.
(b) Paragraph 10A was inserted by S.I. 1988/663 and amended by S.I. 1988/2022, 1989/534, 1990/547 and 1991/503.
(c) Paragraph 10B was inserted by S.I. 1988/663 and amended by S.I. 1989/534 and 1991/503.
(d) Paragraph 10C was inserted by S.I. 1988/2022 and amended by S.I. 1990/547 and 1991/2910.
(e) Paragraph 10D was inserted by S.I. 1989/1678 and amended by S.I. 1990/547.
(f) Paragraph 16 was amended by S.I. 1988/663 and 1445 and 1989/534.
(g) 1948 c.29.
(h) S.I. 1987/1968; the relevant amending instruments are S.I. 1989/136, 1686, and 1991/2284.
(i) *See* regulation 2(1).

(2) In paragraph 4(2) of that Schedule(a), after head (a), there shall be inserted the following head–
"(aa) an amount equal to the amount of any payment the beneficiary is liable to make to the local authority under section 22 of the National Assistance Act 1948(b).".

SCHEDULE 2

Regulation 2(3)

The following Schedule shall be inserted after Schedule 3B of the Income Support Regulations(c):

"SCHEDULE 3C Regulation 2A(1)(b)

THE GREATER LONDON AREA

The area described in this Schedule comprises–

(a) the Boroughs of

Barking	Hillingdon
Barnet	Hounslow
Bexley	Islington
Brent	Kensington and Chelsea
Bromley	Kingston-Upon-Thames
Camden	Lambeth
City of Westminster	Lewisham
Croydon	Merton
Ealing	Newham
Enfield	Redbridge
Greenwich	Richmond-Upon-Thames
Hackney	Southwark
Haringey	Sutton
Hammersmith & Fulham	Tower Hamlets
Harrow	Waltham Forest
Havering	Wandsworth;

(b) the City of London;

(c) in the County of Essex that part of the district of Epping Forest which comprises the parishes of Chigwell and Waltham Holy Cross;

(d) in the County of Hertfordshire, that part of the Borough of Broxbourne which lies south of Cheshunt Park, including Slipe Lane, and that part of the district of Hertsmere which comprises the former parishes of Elstree, Ridge, Shenley and South Mimms;

(e) in the County of Surrey, the Borough of Spelthorne and that part of the Borough of Elmbridge which was formerly administered by the Old Esher District Council."

(a) Paragraph 4(2) was amended by S.I. 1989/136 and 1686.
(b) 1948 c.29; section 22 is extended by the Local Authority Social Services Act 1970 (c.42), s.2(1), Schedule 1; in Scotland subsection (1) was repealed and subsections (2) to (9) applied with modifications by the Social Work (Scotland) Act 1968 (c.49) section 87(3) and (4) and Schedule 9, Part I; section 22 is further amended by section 44(1) to (6) and Schedule 10 to the National Health Service and Community Care Act 1990 (c.19).
(c) Schedule 3B was inserted by S.I. 1989/534.

EXPLANATORY NOTE

(This note is not part of the Regulations)

These Regulations contain amendments arising out of the changes to care in the community which are being introduced on 1st April 1993.

Part II of the Regulations contains amendments to the Income Support (General) Regulations 1987. Regulation 2 introduces a new residential allowance as part of a person's applicable amount in income support for those in residential care homes and nursing homes. Those in such homes before 1st April 1993 are excluded from the new residential allowance for so long as they have a "preserved right" to the higher levels of income support specified in Schedule 4 to the Income Support (General) Regulations 1987. A higher rate of residential allowance is payable in the Greater London Area (regulation 2(3) and Schedule 2).

Those with preserved rights are identified in regulation 3. Part III contains amendments relating to housing benefit. Regulation 4 amends the meaning of residential accommodation in regulation 5 of the Housing Benefit (General) Regulations 1987 so as to provide that references to Part III accommodation relate only to accommodation where board is provided and the premises are owned or managed or owned and managed by a local authority.

Regulation 5 provides that those in residential accommodation who are either in remunerative work or liable to make payments for their accommodation to a close relative will from 1st April 1993 be treated as not liable to make payments in respect of a dwelling. It also preserves existing provisions for such persons who are treated as so liable on 31st March 1993.

Regulation 6 provides that housing benefit is not payable to a person who is provided with board and accommodation by a local authority in an establishment owned or managed or owned and managed by them.

Part V relates to disability benefits. Regulation 7 enables disability living allowance to be payable where the person resides in a hospice or where the person meets the whole of the cost of the accommodation. Regulation 8 makes similar provision in relation to attendance allowance.

Schedule 1 contains a number of amendments to the Income Support (General) Regulations 1987 which arise in consequence of the changes arising on the introduction of community care.

Schedule 2 contains a description of the area in which the higher rate of residential allowance is payable.

The report of the Social Security Advisory Committee dated 11th November 1992 on the draft of these Regulations which had been referred to them, together with a statement giving the response of the Secretary of State to the Committee's recommendations, is contained in Command Paper No. 2115 published by Her Majesty's Stationery Office.

STATUTORY INSTRUMENTS

1992 No. 3147

**SOCIAL SECURITY
HOUSING, ENGLAND AND WALES
HOUSING, SCOTLAND**

The Social Security Benefits (Amendments Consequential Upon the Introduction of Community Care) Regulations 1992

ISBN 0-11-025732-4

£3.10 net
Reprinted 1992
Printed in the United Kingdom for HMSO
880 WO 2393 C20 1/93 51.0.0 56219 ON 227509